Backyard Animals
Rabbits

Annalise Bekkering

Weigl Publishers Inc.

Published by Weigl Publishers Inc.
350 5th Avenue, Suite 3304, PMB 6G
New York, NY 10118-0069
Website: www.weigl.com

Library of Congress Cataloging-in-Publication Data

Bekkering, Annalise.
  Rabbits / Annalise Bekkering.
     p. cm. -- (Backyard animals)
  Includes index.
  ISBN 978-1-59036-679-0 (hard cover : alk. paper) -- ISBN 978-1-59036-680-6 (soft
cover : alk. paper)
  1. Rabbits--Juvenile literature. I. Title.

QL737.L32B45 2008
599.32--dc22

                                                             2006102108

Printed in the United States of America
1 2 3 4 5 6 7 8 9 0 11 10 09 08 07

Editor Heather C. Hudak
Design and Layout Terry Paulhus

Cover: Rabbits live in all parts of the world, except Antarctica.

Contents

Meet the Rabbit

Rabbits are small **mammals** that are covered with fur. They are known for their large ears and short, fluffy tail. Rabbits do not walk like other animals. They hop. They can leap 10 to 15 feet (3 to 4.5 meters).

Rabbits can be gray, brown, black, or white. In nature, they are often hard to see. This is because they can stand still for a long time. The color of their fur blends in with their surroundings, too. Rabbits hide during the day. They feed at night. The darkness hides them from **predators**. Rabbits run and hide when they are in danger. They like to stay close to their shelters.

Rabbits can **adapt** to many places. They live in fields, meadows, farms, and even cities. Rabbits often search for food in gardens.

Rabbits are quiet animals. However, they sometimes scream loudly if they are afraid or hurt.

The mountain cottontail is also known as Nuttall's cottontail. It mainly lives in the western United States.

All about Rabbits

There are 28 different **species** of rabbits in the world. Hares are related to rabbits, but they are not the same.

Some people confuse rabbits and hares. Rabbits are smaller and have shorter ears. Hares are born with hair, and rabbits are born hairless. Hares are able to see at birth, while rabbits are not.

Pet rabbits often live between 7 and 8 years, but some can live for 15 years.

Rabbit Facts

Desert Cottontail

- Climbs trees to use as lookouts
- Can run up to 15 miles (24 kilometers) per hour

Eastern Cottontail

- The most common rabbit in the United States
- Makes tunnels under snow in winter

European Rabbit

- First type of rabbit to be domesticated, or tamed as a pet
- First came from Europe and Africa

Marsh Rabbit

- Hides from predators in water
- Can walk on its hind legs

Mountain Cottontail

- Nests in rocky, bushy areas
- Has shorter ears than other rabbits

Swamp Rabbit

- The largest cottontail rabbit
- An excellent swimmer

Rabbit History

Rabbits came to North America from Asia about 40 million years ago.

There are two main types of rabbits found in nature. These are cottontails and European rabbits. Cottontail rabbits have been in North America for a long time. They are the most common rabbit in North America. A cottontail rabbit's tail looks like a ball of cotton.

European rabbits are also called Old World rabbits. They first lived in Europe and Africa. Most pet rabbits are a type of European rabbit.

People first brought rabbits to Australia and New Zealand around 1860. At first, seven rabbits were released into nature. The population grew quickly. Soon, it became difficult to control.

Mountain cottontails may rest in a form. A form is a bowl-like nest lined with leaves, grass, and fur from the rabbit's belly.

Rabbit Shelter

Rabbits live in forests, deserts, and grasslands. They can live on mountains and in the cold Arctic. Some rabbits live in cities, where they eat lawns and gardens. They find shelter in shrubs.

Most rabbits are social, or friendly, animals. They live with other rabbits in a maze of tunnels called warrens. A warren is an underground den. Rabbit dens can be 10 feet (3 m) deep and can cover a large area. A warren has many entrances, tunnels, and rooms.

Eastern cottontails like to live in open fields with tall grass. They use burrows to protect themselves from cold weather.

Rabbits live near bushes, fences, and brush piles. Some even live under farm equipment, junk, and snowdrifts.

Rabbit Features

Most rabbits are about 1 foot (0.3 m) long and weigh 2 to 3 pounds (0.9 to 1.4 kilograms). Their body is adapted for escaping predators. When faced with danger, rabbits can move quickly.

EYES
A rabbit's eyes are on either side of its head. This allows the rabbit to see a large area. Rabbits can see behind and to the side better than they can see to the front.

NOSE
Rabbits have a keen sense of smell. In nature, they know other rabbits by their smell.

TEETH
Rabbits have large front teeth. They use their teeth to grip and bite plants. Rabbits' teeth are always growing. Gnawing on tough bark wears down their teeth.

EARS

Rabbits have large ears that help them hear well. Their ears can turn. This allows rabbits to hear in all directions.

HIND LEGS

Rabbits have big, strong hind legs. They use their legs to hop, run, and dig tunnels. Rabbits' long legs help them move quickly. They thump their hind leg to warn other rabbits of danger.

What Do Rabbits Eat?

Rabbits are herbivores. They eat plants. In spring, summer, and autumn, rabbits eat grass, leaves, clover, and flowers. In winter, rabbits eat buds, twigs, and bark.

Rabbits like to eat clover. Some gardeners will plant clover near their garden. The rabbits will eat the clover instead of flowers and vegetables.

Rabbits are nocturnal. This means they are most active at night. Rabbits search for food close to their shelter so they can hide if there is danger. They look for food on the ground. Then they rush back into their den, where they rest.

Rabbits living in cities eat flowers, lettuce, carrots, and garden plants.

Rabbits eat weeds and wildflowers,
such as goldenrod and dandelions.

Rabbit Life Cycle

A male rabbit is called a buck. A female rabbit is a doe. Baby rabbits are called kittens, or kits. Most rabbits mate in spring and summer. A doe can have more than 20 kits in one year. Often, kits are born in **litters** of three to eight.

Kits

At birth, kits cannot see or hear. They are hairless. Kits are helpless for up to one week. At one week, kits are covered with soft fur. Two days later, their eyes open, and they can see.

1 Month

Kits leave the den and live on their own when they are about one month old.

A doe makes a nest by digging a form. A mother rabbit visits her kits once every day to feed them. When she leaves, she covers the nest with dirt to protect the kits from danger.

Adult

Rabbits can begin mating when they are four months old. Most rabbits in nature live for about one year. Some live up to two years.

Encountering Rabbits

Rabbits are known to eat crops and gardens. Building a fence will help to keep rabbits away. The fence needs to be at least 2 feet (0.6 m) high. Plastic milk containers with the bottom cut out can be placed over smaller plants as well. Rabbits do not eat all plants. They do not eat flax and marigolds.

If you see an injured rabbit, it is best to call a wildlife officer. If you see kits all alone, it is important not to touch or move them. The mother is likely nearby. A mother rabbit will not care for a kit that has been removed from the nest.

Useful Websites

To learn more about
caring for rabbits, visit:
**www.rabbit.org/faq/sections
/orphan.html**

Rabbits groom often. They use their teeth, tongue, and claws to keep their fur clean.

Myths and Legends

Many cultures have stories and myths about rabbits. Ancient Egyptians worshiped rabbits as a symbol of **fertility**. In some countries, carrying a rabbit's foot is believed to bring good luck.

Some people believe that the **tradition** of the Easter Rabbit began in Germany. A woman hid colored eggs in her garden at Easter. While her children searched for eggs, a hare hopped past. The children thought the hare had left the eggs for them.

Later, German children made nests in their yards for the Easter hare to fill with eggs. German **immigrants** brought this tradition to North America. The Easter hare became known as the Easter Rabbit. This is because rabbits are more common in North America.

The White Rabbit is a character in the Lewis Carroll book *Alice in Wonderland.*

The Legend of the Jade Rabbit

The Jade Rabbit is a Chinese legend about a rabbit that helped some old men.

Three magical wise men begged for food from a fox, a monkey, and a rabbit. The fox and the monkey did not want to share their food.

The rabbit did not have any food. Instead, the rabbit offered himself to the old men. He jumped into the fire to cook himself. The old men were impressed by the rabbit. They put out the fire. The men allowed the rabbit to live in a palace on the Moon. There, he became the Jade Rabbit. Today, the Jade Rabbit can still be seen in the Moon.

Frequently Asked Questions

How can I tell if rabbits visit my backyard?

Answer: If rabbits visit your backyard, you might see tracks in the dirt or snow. Flowers or vegetables in a garden might be eaten.

Do other animals hunt rabbits in nature?

Answer: Rabbits have many predators. Hawks, owls, foxes, raccoons, skunks, and opossums are some of the animals that hunt rabbits.

Can rabbits swim?

Answer: All rabbits will swim to escape predators. Some, such as the swamp rabbit, swim to move from one place to another. If a rabbit is being hunted, it will stay under water. Only its nose will remain above the water.

Puzzler

Find out how much you know about rabbits.

1. How long do rabbits live in nature?
2. What are three different types of rabbits?
3. How can you protect your garden from rabbits?
4. What do rabbits eat?
5. How do rabbits warn other rabbits of danger?

Answers: 1. one to two years **2.** desert cottontail, eastern cottontail, European rabbit, marsh rabbit, mountain cottontail, and swamp rabbit **3.** build a fence, or plant clover near the garden **4.** grass, vegetables, bark, leaves, clover, and flowers **5.** by thumping their hind leg

Find Out More

There are many different stories and books about rabbits. Look for these and other books at your library.

DK Publishing. *Watch Me Grow: Rabbit.* Dorling Kindersley, 2004.

Swanson, Diane. *Welcome to the World of Rabbits and Hares.* Walrus Books, 2000.

Words to Know

adapt: to adjust to the natural environment

fertility: the ability to produce young

immigrants: people who leave one country to live in another

litters: a group of animals born to one mother at the same time

mammals: animals that have fur, make milk, and are born live

predators: animals that hunt and eat other animals for food

species: a group of animals or plants that have many features in common

tradition: a custom or belief that is passed on

Index